SandCastle 3

Homonyms

Line Up on the Line

Kelly Doudna

ABDO
Publishing Company

Published by SandCastle™, an imprint of ABDO Publishing Company, 4940 Viking Drive, Edina, Minnesota 55435.

Printed in the United States.

Photo credits: Artville, Comstock, Corbis Images, Eyewire Images, Image 100, PhotoDisc, Rubberball Productions

Library of Congress Cataloging-in-Publication Data

Doudna, Kelly, 1963-
     Line up on the line / Kelly Doudna.
       p. cm. -- (Homonyms)
     Includes index.
     Summary: Photographs and simple text introduce homonyms, words that are spelled and sound the same but have different meanings.
     ISBN 1-57765-787-X
      1. English language--Homonyms--Juvenile literature. [1. English language--Homonyms.] I. Title.

PE1595 .D75 2002
428.1--dc21

2001053370

The SandCastle concept, content, and reading method have been reviewed and approved by a national advisory board including literacy specialists, librarians, elementary school teachers, early childhood education professionals, and parents.

Let Us Know

After reading the book, SandCastle would like you to tell us your stories about reading. What is your favorite page? Was there something hard that you needed help with? Share the ups and downs of learning to read. We want to hear from you! To get posted on the Abdo Publishing Company Web site, send us email at:

sandcastle@abdopub.com

About SandCastle™

Nonfiction books for the beginning reader

- Basic concepts of phonics are incorporated with integrated language methods of reading instruction. Most words are short, and phrases, letter sounds, and word sounds are repeated.

- Book levels are based on the ATOS™ for Books formula. Other considerations for readability include the number of words in each sentence, the number of characters in each word, and word lists based on curriculum frameworks.

- Full-color photography reinforces word meanings and concepts.

- "Words I Can Read" list at the end of each book teaches basic elements of grammar, helps the reader recognize the words in the text, and builds vocabulary.

- Reading levels are indicated by the number of flags on the castle.

SandCastle uses the following definitions for this series:

- Homographs: words that are spelled the same but sound different and have different meanings. *Easy memory tip: "-graph"= same look*

- Homonyms: words that are spelled and sound the same but have different meanings. *Easy memory tip: "-nym"= same name*

- Homophones: words that sound alike but are spelled differently and have different meanings. *Easy memory tip: "-phone"= sound alike*

Look for more SandCastle books in these three reading levels:

Level 1 (one flag)	**Level 2** (two flags)	**Level 3** (three flags)

Grades Pre-K to K 5 or fewer words per page	**Grades K to 1** 5 to 10 words per page	**Grades 1 to 2** 10 to 15 words per page

lock

lock

Homonyms are words that are spelled and sound the same but have different meanings.

We wait for the school bus.

We are the last ones to get on.

I have a big lollipop.

It will last a long time.

It is autumn.

We have fun playing in the leaves.

My friend leaves school at the same time I do.

We walk home together.

I am doing my homework.

I write with my left hand.

I bought a cupcake.

It was the last one left.

We played all afternoon.

We will lie here and rest for a while.

I like to tell the truth.

It is not nice to lie.

A feather does not weigh much.

It is very light.

I like to read.

I can see better in the bright light.

Dad holds me up while I shoot the basket.

I long to grow taller.

My brother has very short hair.

My hair is very long.

My dog had babies.

She has four puppies in her litter.

My cat knows where to go.

He uses his litter box.

I want to make the swim team.

I will swim a lap to practice.

I slid down the slide with my puppy.

Where did he sit?

(lap)

Words I Can Read

Nouns

A noun is a person, place, or thing

afternoon
(af-tur-NOON) p. 12
autumn (AW-tuhm) p. 8
babies (BAY-beez) p. 18
basket (BASS-kit) p. 16
brother (BRUHTH-ur)
p. 17
cat (KAT) p. 19
cupcake (KUHP-kayk)
p. 11
dog (DAWG) p. 18
feather (FETH-ur) p. 14
friend (FREND) p. 9
fun (FUHN) p. 8
hair (HAIR) p. 17
hand (HAND) p. 10

homework
(HOME-wurk) p. 10
homonyms
(HOM-uh-nimz) p. 5
lap (LAP) pp. 20, 21
leaves (LEEVZ) p. 8
light (LITE) p. 15
litter (LIT-ur) p. 18
litter box
(LIT-ur BOKS) p. 19
lock (LOK) p. 4
lollipop (LOL-ee-pop)
p. 7
meanings (MEE-ningz)
p. 5
much (MUHCH) p. 14

one (WUHN) p. 11
ones (WUHNZ) p. 6
puppies (PUHP-eez)
p. 18
puppy (PUHP-ee) p. 21
school (SKOOL) p. 9
school bus
(SKOOL BUHSS) p. 6
slide (SLIDE) p. 21
swim team
(SWIM TEEM) p. 20
time (TIME) pp. 7, 9
truth (TROOTH) p. 13
while (WILE) p. 12
words (WURDZ) p. 5

Proper Nouns

A proper noun is the name of a
person, place, or thing

Dad (DAD) p. 16

Pronouns

A pronoun is a word that replaces a noun

he (HEE) pp. 19, 21
I (EYE) pp. 7, 9, 10, 11,
13, 15, 16, 20, 21

it (IT) pp. 7, 8, 11, 13, 14
me (MEE) p. 16
she (SHEE) p. 18

that (THAT) p. 5
we (WEE) pp. 6, 8, 9, 12

Verbs

A verb is an action or being word

am (AM) p. 10
are (AR) pp. 5, 6
bought (BAWT) p. 11
can (KAN) p. 15
did (DID) p. 21
do (DOO) p. 9
does (DUHZ) p. 14
doing (DOO-ing) p. 10
get (GET) p. 6
go (GOH) p. 19
grow (GROH) p. 16
had (HAD) p. 18
has (HAZ) pp. 17, 18
have (HAV) pp. 5, 7, 8
holds (HOHLDZ) p. 16
is (IZ) pp. 8, 13, 14, 17

knows (NOHZ) p. 19
last (LAST) p. 7
leaves (LEEVZ) p. 9
left (LEFT) p. 11
lie (LYE) pp. 12, 13
like (LIKE) pp. 13, 15
long (LAWNG) p. 16
make (MAYK) p. 20
played (PLAYD) p. 12
playing (PLAY-ing) p. 8
practice (PRAK-tiss)
   p. 20
read (REED) p. 15
rest (REST) p. 12
see (SEE) p. 15

shoot (SHOOT) p. 16
sit (SIT) p. 21
slid (SLID) p. 21
sound (SOUND) p. 5
spelled (SPELD) p. 5
swim (SWIM) p. 20
tell (TEL) p. 13
uses (YOOZ-ez) p. 19
wait (WATE) p. 6
walk (WAWK) p. 9
want (WONT) p. 20
was (WUHZ) p. 11
weigh (WAY) p. 14
will (WIL) pp. 7, 12, 20
write (RITE) p. 10

Adjectives

An adjective describes something

all (AWL) p. 12
better (BET-ur) p. 15
big (BIG) p. 7
bright (BRITE) p. 15
different (DIF-ur-uhnt)
   p. 5
four (FOR) p. 18
her (HUR) p. 18

his (HIZ) p. 19
last (LAST) pp. 6, 11
left (LEFT) p. 10
light (LITE) p. 14
long (LAWNG) pp. 7, 17
my (MYE)
   pp. 9, 10, 17, 18, 19, 21

nice (NEYESS) p. 13
same (SAYM) pp. 5, 9
short (SHORT) p. 17
taller (TAWL-ur) p. 16
up (UHP) p. 16

Adverbs

An adverb tells how, when, or where
something happens

down (DOUN) p. 21

here (HIHR) p. 12

home (HOME) p. 9

not (NOT) pp. 13, 14

together
(tuh-GETH-ur) p. 9

very (VER-ee) pp. 14, 17

where (WAIR) p. 21